FARMLANDIA.

The Many Lives of a Florida Farm

Virginia Aronson

PART 1.

Elizabeth Ryan, Florida, 1878

*The great inevitability of defeat must be met
with dignity and beauty.*
                        —Leonard Cohen

One blond day
sunlight a flickering glow
through the leafy trees
the blushing color of
a new peach
Laney said it was time
to head out
they packed up
all of their belongings
the work boots and raingear
the dresses and shawls
the pillows and bed things
her Dutch oven—
a cast-iron pot
on little black feet—
blackened skillets
kitchen knives, coal oil lamps
his Bowie knife, his tools
rifle and shells
all the lovely baby clothes
she had been making
and soon after
he lifted her up
and set her down
on the hard seat
upfront
in the loaded buckboard
he untied Joade
the gray mule
he giddy-upped Kate
the coffee brown horse
and off they went.

The tears came fast

as they drove away
as they were leaving
everything Elizabeth loved
leaving Georgia
the four hundred acre peach farm
where they had lived
where Laney grew up
where he had worked
his whole life
leaving Arcadia
her sweet little town
the only home
she had ever known
leaving her family
they visited on Sundays
when they went in town
for services
leaving the church
where she was baptized
leaving her friends
young girls like her
with husbands and babies
homes and work to do
making a nice life
making families
leaving everything
she knew in the world—
for what?

For the great unknown.

For Laney's dream
for free land
for an unknown land
for the Southern Frontier:

Florida.

He told her, *It's warm there*
all year long
and we can grow
oranges!
pineapples!
mangos!

Laine Patrick Ryan
knew all about
the value
of fresh food.
A sickly child
abandoned unwanted
Irish orphan
he'd been taken in
by Christian farmers
the good people
of Arcadia
fed him, gave him
a home, schooling
and he built up
his scrawny body
with hard work
and fresh food.

He wanted to make her see
how this would work
for them too
for their children.
He wanted their own farm
and promised his wife
they would thrive
eating grapefruit

limes and lemons
little bananas
fresh melons
juicy berries
all the fruit
they grew themselves
in big fruitful groves
and soon enough
they would sit together
on the front porch
of their farm, their home
with their children
watching the trees
bear fruit
and she would see
them prosper and grow
their bounty and they would
survive and thrive.

When he talked like this
she swallowed the nausea—
fear that his dreams
would grow into a garden
of her own regrets—
banished her thoughts
to smile at him
her handsome husband
his hair a red flame
above his sweet freckled face.
She had no say
so she said nothing
held him close
in her heart.

They would follow his dreams

and she would pray:
that the baby did not come
too early
that the baby would come
nice and easy—
no doctor
no midwife
just Laney
and Elizabeth—
that she could
birth this baby
so that
there would be more—
more babies
more love
more hands
to help them
grow fruit
grow produce
grow the farm
grow and survive, thrive
in the great unknown
Florida.

It's been many days now
on the road
the sky sharply bluer
white clouds bigger
fluffy balls of cotton
she can almost touch
as they drive on
a slow trot in the hot
sear of sunshine, endless
heat, endless harsh
light, that blinding light

Georgia behind them
Florida in front of them
brush and bramble
as far as they can see
but not far enough
south
for Laney to stop
to settle in.

Not yet, Laney says
each night
when they stretch out
under the crickets' chirp
the pine trees' sway
the soft wind
to try to sleep
until just before dawn.

Almost there, he promises
in the barest light
when he lifts her up
when she mounts the buckboard
once again
for the long hard drive
the road ruts
the mosquitos
the fast heavy rains
the mud and muck
day after day
the pre-dawn morning
the single blessing
a touch of coolness
in the thick shroud
of trapped heat.

It's early
April and already
days so hot
the world is dazed
languid, the scent
of baking greenery
permeates the air
she is unable
to imagine
the discomfort
of days to come
in May
in June
in July
in August
and the fleets of insects
sand flies and gnats
fat flies, mosquitos
swarm
bite
fill her eyes
her mouth and nose.
Kate snorts and shakes
her big brown head
Joade kicks a bit
when the snakes slither past
startling at the flash and blinker
when the darkness blips
with lightning bugs.

Still, they suffer and drive
carry on
on and on and on
her ruined traveling dress
soaked through with sweat

she will have to tear it
for scraps
when they get
to wherever
they are going
to land.

She bounces and bangs
on the hardwood seat
on the bumpy dirt road
in the strange wilderness
searching for the flora
in Flora-da
but finds no flowers—
only scrub pines and spiked bushes
thick groves of rangy brush
cypress trees in low water
with roots like knees
sticking up from the brackish
green brown sludge.

The farther south they go
the deeper in jungle
they venture
the more scared
she becomes,
barely sixteen
and six months along
and suddenly her life
a nerve-racking journey
into the wild unknown.

But this is what she pledged
to make of her life

when she married
Laine Patrick Ryan
the good looking older man
who spotted her
in the church choir
one Sunday
came to see her father
the next
the man sitting astride
a dusty mule
behind her
the man who will dismount
walk for endless miles
to give their Joade
a needed rest
the man who calls up
to her
to ask
how she is
and cares
how she answers.

Laney has told her
how it will be
while they set up
the farm:
he will hunt wild
hogs and deer
for the meat
smaller animals
for meat and fur
ducks and turtles
quail and turkeys
to sell or barter
he will travel

to the nearest settlement
on the nearest river
where the steamers stop
where he can trade
for their supplies
to build their home.
Laney says not to worry
we will catch the rainwater
and live near a creek
we will have all the meat
we can eat, wild greens
we can find, wild berries
we can pick...
He tells her
his face sad
they must go without
his most beloved
fresh-picked fruits
and vegetables
peaches and rhubarb
lettuce and carrots
potatoes, onions—
but just for a time
and time
is what we have
Laney says
many times.

He is full of confidence
in himself
in the land
in the South
in Florida
he says it is all
a matter of time.

Elizabeth says
but only to herself:
what is time
when your belly grows larger
your breath shorter
your heart speeding up
alone in its bone cage?

The sun has set
in a bright orange bowl
as darkness seeps
into the blue-black sky
into the rainbow wash
they pull over
for the night
off the dirt road
made by soldiers
during the Seminole wars.

For days and days
they've been alone
no one else around
no other travelers
no signs of life
but the wildlife:
fluttering raptors
swooping hawks
little kestrel falcons
an occasional owl
skydiving
for their dinnertime meals.
They've heard rustling
in the thick brush
they've passed by

big black alligators
big black snakes
sunning themselves
in the road.
They've seen
bobcats and panthers
fleeing deer
all kinds of strange animals
with spikes and prongs
scales and fangs
that look nothing like
Georgia wildlife.

When night shuts
its broad dark curtain
the glowing eyes
and empty howl
of wolves nearby
make Elizabeth curl up close
to her husband
to the embers
of their fire.

Tonight they make camp
in a copse, a hammock
of leafless trees
long thin branches strung
with giant spiders
with gold silk webs
tree limbs speckled
with beady-eyed crows
watching them
planning an invasion
of their simple rest stop
beside a gurgling creek

she longs to bathe
in the cool water
cleanse her
dust-crusted
mud-spattered
sunburned
patchy red skin
but is too exhausted
to undress.

Laney makes a smudge pot
in a tin can
with mangrove sap
to keep off the bugs
while they eat hardtack
salt pork and jerky
roast biscuits
on sticks
over the low fire
and they split
the last of the mushy peaches
then lie down together
under the wide bare branches.

She misses the sweet smell
of magnolia blossoms
a perfume she once splashed
on her soft pale skin—
no more.

Laney talks nonstop
and she allows
his deep voice
to relax
her aching muscles

to rock
her worried mind
to a still, soothed
calm.

He tells her about
the Indian land
they are on
sacred land
that must be treated
with respect,
all of Florida
Indian land
the Spanish claimed
for their own
killing off tribes
with guns and sickness—
Timucuans gone
Ais and Calusas
Apalachees
Creek
Tequestas.

Laney tells her how
British soldiers came next
fought three bloody wars
until the native Seminoles
moved into the swampland
where they still live
in chickee huts
made of cypress poles
palmetto thatch roofs,
he says they live well
hunt and fish and grow
lots of good food

because they understand
the harsh wilderness
their sacred land
Florida.

Indians know how
to make a life
in the swamp.

Laney tells her
how they too will survive
thrive on their land,
land
they will respect
land
that will provide for them:
he will shoot
the pure white
egret and ibis
beautiful birds
they can eat
trading the feathers
(the plumes in demand
for ladies' hats);
he will shoot raccoons
skin them, dry
their pelts
on frames
in the sun
for furs to trade
for a guinea cow
for her
for her milk
and butter

for a pair of oxen
to help him
work the land;
he will catch and tame
wild horses,
the ones left behind
by Spanish soldiers
beautiful horses that wander
acres of unclaimed land,
land he will claim
for their farm
land he will fence
for a small herd
of horses
he knows she will
love.

Her mind drifts and she sees
uniformed soldiers
young boys riding
the big brown animals
so young, so alive
until *boom!*
shot from the saddle
they fall by the road
their horses fleeing
into the brush.

She shifts her legs
rolls toward Laney
the baby kicking
their hearts in sync
she breathes deep
begins to fade.

Laney tells her how
he will trade
pretty snakeskins
and the skin of wild cows
to the merchant
at the settlement
closest to their land,
he will trade there
for a hound dog
to herd cattle
all the wild cows
he can fatten up
and graze west
to the cattle market
to sell for gold.

She tries to listen
to Laney's stories
tries to imagine
sweet-smelling citrus
figs
guavas
paw-paw
inhale the earthy aroma
from a garden full of greens
bright red tomatoes
orange melons
yellow squash
fat pumpkins
the sweet wood smell
of the home he will build
from oaks, pine, palm
with a front porch
for rocking chairs

their feet up
as the brilliant sunsets
of their prosperous days
bloody their land
and they watch beauty
spread like golden honey
on their farm, their land
with their children
their animals
their own bright-lit
futures.

Their own land
Florida land—
Farmlandia.

His dreams so vast
she cannot picture them all
no room in her head
for visions that big:
bigger than wild cows
bigger than wild horses
bigger than black gators
spiders, snakes, everything
she fears might be
lying in wait.

The baby kicks again
and she falls
into a dream
she is two people
or one huge one
floating, floating
somewhere
lost in time

lost in the great wild
the great unknown:
she takes a deep breath
water shoots from the spout
at the top of her head

she holds her breath
and goes under.

Travel Biscuits

2 cups flour
4 tsp. baking powder
¾ tsp. salt
6 tbsp. fat (lard or butter)

1. In a bowl, mix all ingredients together using a fork; keep batter crumbly.
2. Roll batter on lightly floured board to ¼-inch thickness.
3. Cut into small rounds using the top of a water glass. Set on a greased baking sheet.
4. Bake in a very hot oven 12-14 minutes or until golden brown.
5. Pack in a cloth napkin for easy carry.

To cook over a campfire, do not roll out. Simply wrap the stiff batter around a stick and roast until golden brown. Slide off the stick and fill the hole with butter, syrup or jam.

PART 2.

Elsa Ryan, Farmlandia, 1895

Florida is a strange place: hot, beautiful, ugly.
I love it here, and how nothing makes sense
but still, somehow, there is a rhythm.
                              —Roxanne Gay

Darkness holds me close
as weak morning light
fills me with unbearable longing
to stay wrapped in the blanket
to stay warm, held, loved.

I get up.
The cows need milking
my dreams need forgetting.

I am a dreamy girl, not yet
a woman
but with a man's
burdens, the farm
my responsibility
my little brother
has no one else now
just me and the animals.

Leaving the crinkly comfort
of my palmetto-stuffed bed
I rise quick
dress hurriedly
in the cold dark
this chill the Florida
version of winter—
mild but biting
in contrast to the usual
endless balm of heat,
heat, heat, heat.

The air today is glass
I can see everything.

I cannot take care of
this farm by myself,
not if we want to grow. We must
grow
if we are to survive—
Papa told me this
so many times
it is a song now
in my head:
grow and survive
grow to survive
grow, grow, grow
survive and thrive.

I pull on Papa's old blue
workshirt and worry, worry
I don't want to end up
in West Palm
in a tumbledown shack
another poor woman
with a passel of kids
and nothing else
to call her own.
I don't want to work
at the Royal Poinciana Hotel
cleaning rooms, cleaning up
for the rich—
not when I can work here
for myself, for us
our garden, our groves, our land
homesteaded by Papa
and Mama
and I want this land
to stay ours.

Our land
our rich land.

I dress in a long cotton skirt
Mama's old boots
hot and scratchy most of the year
but necessary today:
it's cold enough this morning
been chilly all week
a big change
the animals don't like
they shiver, blood thin
from being raised here
in the year-round swelter
the thick humidity.
Not today
air so cold, so dry
I am grateful
I thought to cover
the vegetable garden
with grain sacks
wrap all the citrus trees
from the possibility
of a dusting
of frost.

I brush out my long hair
braid it tight
pin it up
thinking about the garden:
not much growing now
but in the spring
my brother Donal
will help me
plant more

beans, corn, squash.
We did real good
with tomatoes last year
our pumpkins huge
our melons too
and someday
we'll live real good
off the profits
from our land
we'll sit on the porch
our feet up, watching
our future
grow
on trees—
guava, banana
mango, papaya
sugar apple
sour orange
alligator pear
these kinds
of semi-tropical trees
I can plant
in the groves
of citrus trees
Papa and Mama planted
and now it's my own
responsibility
to grow,
grow more.

The kitchen cold and dark
I don't want to light
the stove just yet.
I grab two milk buckets
from their place

near the big iron
potbellied stove
and head outside

my breath steams
makes circles in the frigid air
like Papa's smoke rings.

A duck limps up
squawking, her head
nodding, nodding
and I lean down low
to pet my peg-leg pet
duck, sweet bird
following me around
as a tiny duckling
all yellow fluff
and squeaky bill
one crippled leg
marking her
an outsider
mine to care for
Peg will follow me
to the barn.

In the distance, a pair
perfect and still
sandhill cranes posed
each one balanced
on one twiggy leg,
a circling hawk
lands on the furry branch
of a lean pine tree
settles in to wait
for mice to show themselves.

In the distance, a V:
long flight of herons
leaving behind rookeries
heading farther south
where the air is warmer.

Chilled now
through my thin
Florida clothes
I hurry across hard-packed dirt
listening to an eerie owl
hoot, hoot
heading to where
the cows wait patiently
for a pair of milking hands.

I am grateful
Mama taught me how
to milk
before she got sick she knew
I would need her skills
she knew she would never
recover, blood loss
from childbirth
energy drained
from farm work
no doctors, no help
except Papa
and me
she showed me everything
she'd learned
taking care of
the farm.

When Donal started walking

Mama stopped walking
took to the big bed
never got up again.
Papa stopped laughing
didn't cry either
his face crumpled up
he went out to the edge
of the fences
they built together
he went out there alone
this time
dug the hole
under the big banyan tree.

The same spot
we buried Flora
the old cow dog
all the barn cats
I'll be buried there
one day too.

The barn is warm
and smells of cows
and their leavings
I breathe in
rich animal odor
the hot aroma of life
on our land. A farm is
a whole world
my whole world
a deep, all-encompassing world

so much responsibility

thinking about it
scares me.

Donal was mine to raise
Papa said after
Mama went in the ground
and we stood for a while
looking down
at the sandy dirt
and the milk cows were mine
he said
his freckled face
unsmiling, thin shoulders
more narrow
than they'd been before—
he seemed to be
shrinking
Elsa
he said,
you got to keep on taking care
of the chickens too.

Chickens are dumb
nervous birds, flighty
anxious, twitchy
they'll nip you
for no reason
fly in your face, wings flapping
you have to feed them grass
when they won't bother
to get off their nests
instead of being grateful
they'll peck you
their manure smells
I hate mucking out

the coop
to spread on the fields.
I don't like them
the guinea hens
the laying hens
but the baby chicks
downy, adorable
and when they hatch
they still have a sac
the rest of the yolk
they came from
tucked inside
their bellies
pulled inside
eventually
after feeding them
the first few days,
nature so strange
and wondrous.

Donal is responsible
for the chickens now
I hated being in charge
glad every time
Papa killed one
so I could make us
chicken dinner.

That day by the grave
the clouds marched in
grey precision, thunderheads
close enough to reach up
and grab, push aside
Donal wandered off
hunting for prey

little green lizards
that run up and down
lumpy roots, peeling bark
I watched him, my heart
clenching like a fist
inside my chest
I could milk
and gather eggs, feed
the animals and water them
but I didn't know how
to mother
a little boy.
How could I
do all the things
Mama had done
and still grow up
myself?

It seemed to me
an impossible request
but it wasn't
a request
my life changed
to one of necessity
suddenly
an adult.

Donal would grow up
fast
too—
how we would both
survive.

Warm now
in the midst

of the soft-breathing animals
I reach for the hand-carved milking stool
carry it to the cows.

What Papa hadn't told me
that day by the grave
was how all the other chores
I'd taken on
for a sick Mama
would continue
to be mine
because he knew
I already knew
what I would be responsible for:
cooking
cleaning
washing
sewing and mending
fetching firewood
from the brush
fetching rainwater
from the cistern,
creek, pond
weeding the garden
harvesting the crops
preserving the food
salting and drying meat—
rabbits, squirrels
raccoons and possum
whatever got hunted
we ate with dinner
we ate with supper too
with beans or split peas
hoe johnny or grits

swamp cabbage or pokeweed
same food, same meal
twice a day,
day after day
the woodpile
the buttonwood fire
the hot flames
cooking, cooking
and cleaning up after

all the chores
sunup to sundown
and into the dark
night after night—
responsibility
scared me then
scares me now.

I sit on the stool
Peg nestles in
beside me
Bodie turns to look
at me
big eyes wide
chews her cud
waiting patiently
waiting
for me
to ease her full udder
to do what needs to be done
she puts herself in my hands
every morning, every evening
without a struggle
wise Bodie
knows I struggle with

knowing, accepting—
she is my cow
this is my land
everything I touch
is my own
responsibility.

When Papa died
last spring
from a lingering illness
from the influenza
I was ill too
we were all sick
for weeks, weak
when I was able
to climb out of bed
I dug the hole
and thought about
what death meant
on our farm:
assigning my brother
some of my chores
so I could do Papa's.

Donal can't milk yet,
his hands not strong
but he does
what he can—
fishing the creek
for redfish
for snook
for catfish
big and ugly
but they taste so good
with fresh churned butter

slices of lemons
like the bullfrog legs
Donal catches
he's pretty handy
with the rifle too
so we eat our share
of raccoon meat
of rabbit stew
possum stew
venison stew.

Sometimes we'll go
over to the coast
on hot afternoons
to catch the breeze
fish in the brackish water
of the silent inlet
brimming with mullet.

Sometimes we take
a full day trip
across the water
in a skiff
to the island quiet
to the coconut beach
the whisper of tides
stroking the shoreline
the white sugar sand
blinding in the sun.

Our pale skin burns
but we enjoy this
freedom
picking up shells
tiny ones, giant ones

pink and pearly gray
dotted and striped pretty
big conch
for conch chowder
we chase horseshoe crabs
for crab soup
we dig turtle eggs
for omelets
we dig oysters
for oyster stew.

We watch the sandpipers
running on tiny legs
pelicans swooping
in formation
inches above waves
thick with fleeing fish
Donal knee-deep
in warm tidal froth
fishing, fishing
for the big king mackerel
he never catches.

I wait in the shade
of the sea grape trees
their leafy branches
I shake out
collect a bucket
of sea grapes
we can take home
turn into jelly.
This land no one owns—
it feeds us well.

Softly now
I clean off
Bodie's teats
she lets me
trusting me
to be gentle with her
as she is with me—
maybe this is love.

She shifts her flank,
all calmness
gratitude
her heavy udders
must weigh on her
day after day
filling
with thick creamy milk.
She's always the first
to be milked
lets me lean my face
on her furry flank
without moving away
from my touch
or whipping me
with a tail
crusted over
with straw
and manure.

Her lucid brown eyes
gaze at me
placidly
like I'm a friend
she allows
to come close

to relieve her
of the burden
of being female
on a farm.

I smile at my sweet cow
her warm liquid hitting
the metal bucket
a rewarding *splat*
I close my eyes
and squeeze, squeeze
in the twice daily
milking rhythm
our work in tandem
and I drift off
to the world beyond
this small farm
this little plot
of cultivated land
in the middle of nowhere—
the Atlantic ten miles
east
the Gulf more
than a hundred miles
west
and what lies beyond
those sandy beaches
those vast blue bodies
of salty water
I have no idea
I will not see
I could never abandon
what Mama and Papa
worked for
died for—

our home
our land.

My parents made the trek
to find land and
claimed it
tamed it
named it
Farmlandia
Mama painted the sign
Papa hung the sign
from the pond apple tree
where the dirt road meets
our front walk
to our small house
he built
the walls
from fresh cut logs
one room: kitchen
living and sleeping
in a simple cabin
he created rafters
and crossbeams
wooden shutters
a thatched roof
from palm fronds
he made a path
to our door
smooth fieldstones
Mama lined
with wildflowers.

After I came
Papa added the porch
where we could sit

in rocking chairs
in the shade
he built us
a separate storeroom
for food and supplies
when Donal was due
a back addition—
two more rooms
for dining and sleeping
he remade the roof
sturdy cypress shingles
our farm growing,
growing to survive.

My parents risked it all
worked hard
struggled, suffered
and died young
for this land
sacred land
nobody else wanted.

Nobody wanted the land
for many reasons—
heat and humidity
endless sand hills
impenetrable scrub
spiky sawgrass
Spanish bayonet
sharp as knives
hammocks scattered
in uninviting clots
knotty cabbage palms
with difficult fruit
deep dark muck

deep dark swamps
full of black sinkholes
big spiders, giant webs
six-foot indigo snakes
deadly rattlesnakes
the screams of panthers
the bellows of gators—
twelve-foot alligators
coming to the swamp
in the dry season
to hibernate
leaving in wet summer
able to sprint
faster than us.

Papa could see
beyond the daily hardships
to something else entirely:
a land of vast beauty
wild orchids perched
on strangler fig vines
like long thick ropes
tangling up tall trees,
bromeliads and air ferns
flowering frangipani
pink and white buds
morning glory vines
dripping purple flowers
poinciana trees dropping
bright red blossoms
scattered like confetti
thick white moon vines
blooming at night
on the brick-red bark
of gumbo limbos

the thick jungle cling
the wild hair growth
sweetsop and soursop
serene green ponds
dotted with little coots
tall skinny rails
wood storks and limpkins
huge eagles perched
in bare mangrove branches

a land rich with life
a land bountiful
a land fruitful
with potential
for a good life
for his family.

Papa saw gator hide sales
where Mama saw danger
he imagined gator tail meat
where she felt only fear
he worshipped the beauty
she knew the hard work.

Papa was excited:
nobody around for miles
they could have as much
open land
as they could farm
as they could plant trees on
as far
as the eye could see.

Papa thought
we were far enough south

we wouldn't have to worry
about winter
frosts…

He was wrong. Still:
what they made of scrub and sand
is indeed fruitful
is indeed bountiful
is indeed rich—
our citrus trees give oranges
and lemons
grapefruit, limes
we grow pineapples
wild berries everywhere
and pokeweed to boil
for bitter greens
coontie and cattails
(native plants we grind
to flour for bread)
our garden plentiful
most of the year
and in the short winters
when fresh food runs out
pantry supplies
jams and jellies
stewed tomatoes and beans
steamed squash and green peppers
corn for mush, grits
sweet buttered cornbread.

The cold fronts come in
fast
leave quick
sweetening up collards
making our oranges juicier

the sun asserting itself
again and we go out
Donal and I
climb ladders
in the chill air, toss
the fat orange globes
like ice balls, hard
into our grain sacks
eat some right there
frosted fruit off the tree.

I remove my face
from the warm comfort
of our little guinea cow
from the welcome respite
of dreams and memories.
The bucket is full
her udder drained
I pet her soft ears
and she nuzzles my neck.

Next up, her offspring
cow of a different nature:
Boo, born on the farm
I watched her slide out
of her mama's fat belly
stand up on spindly legs.
Papa said he was glad
she was a girl
we had no use for a male
calf on the farm.
What would he have done
with a boy,
shoot it?

I didn't ask, I was
so young
so naïve
about the harsh realities
of farm life
back then
I'd wanted to be friends
with the new calf
but Boo balked
hyper and flighty, scared
and now
she's a stubborn cow
and we fight
over who's in charge and
some days she's the boss
kicks over the milk bucket
to prove it.

When I approach her
she eyes me
with distaste
I say, *Boo*
you got to let me work
with you
not against you

like Papa used to say
Mama too.

I'm wary ever since
that one time
I wasn't paying attention
Boo kicked me
square in the ribs
my chest on fire

blue-black for weeks
my breath catching
whenever I moved
so now I know
to tie her tail
to one of the posts
that hold up the barn roof
or she'll whip me mercilessly
and I'll go back to the house
covered in gooey blobs
of her fresh manure.

You look like crap, Elsa,
Donal says, laughing.

I let him say such things
he's a boy
a growing boy
with no parents
no schooling
just me
and the animals
our land.

I carry the buckets
though the icy air
to the house
Peg behind me
hobbling along
squawking along
and Donal runs up
his long hair messy
from sleep
smelling like chickens
so I know

he's already done
this morning's chores
he takes one
of the heavy pails
his hair sticking out
in all directions
like black straw.

The air is glass
I can still see
everything.

We carry the buckets inside
the stove going
and the warmth
he made for us
makes me smile
my stomach growling
I wish I'd gone
to the storage shed
for the Mason jars
beans, jam, fruit preserves
for the last few days
we've been eating only
milk, eggs, the grits
Papa called *sofkee*
made with syrup
from our cane patch
or with cracklin'
(fried and salted
pork rind)
from wild hog meat
Papa put up
his last winter.

After tossing handfuls
of hard corn
to my impatient duck
I wash up
in the tin tub
eye the pale blue
and brown and tan
eggs
piled up high
in a full basket
still hen-warm.

I'm so hungry for eggs,
Donal jokes
his high giggle
contagious and I laugh too—
we amuse each other
the way Papa taught us:
we flip through
the Sears catalogue
marveling at items
we will never own,
we play Hearts
on long cold nights,
we shoot marbles
when the kitchen's warm
and chores are done
I love to let
my little brother win.

Donal keeps it light
looks on the funny side
while I tend to brood
which I do too much
now

it's just us
on the land
on the farm
Farmlandia
me and Donal
alone out here
in the barren winter
in middle of nowhere
Florida.

Sofkee

hardwood ash
cracked corn
optional: sugar syrup
optional: cracklin'

1. Put cold water in a deep pot. Add ash and corn in equal amounts.
2. Bring to a boil over high heat; turn to low and cook until soft, stirring with a wooden spoon.
3. When corn is brown, remove from heat. Add flavorings, if desired.
4. Serve hot as a soup or cold like pudding.

PART 3.

Elsa Ryan, Farmlandia, 1960

54

The farmer has to be an optimist
or he wouldn't still be a farmer.
—*Will Rogers*

Another glorious spring
evening, sun slow
dancing to the horizon
garden shimmering green
buzzing with fat bees
butterflies, crawling things
birds nestling or feasting
buds singing, sprouting
new life set before me
like a bountiful dinner plate
served up to me
alone
sitting on the front porch
bare feet propped up
yellow, knobbed
rough hands worn
tucked away in pockets
eyes blurred, dimming
mind like a TV screen
vivid scenes in review
the years in review.

The years have passed
as they do
but I'm still here
I keep going
I keep Farmlandia
going.

Over the years
my little brother
Donal experienced life
out in the world—
love, women, travel
work that made him happy

while I kept the farm
I kept the farm going
I kept Farmlandia
going, going
sometimes alone
sometimes with help
once with love—
not for long
not for a lifetime.

Over the years
the state kept growing
around Farmlandia
this area they called
Prairie
even though
there was no prairie
over the years
people moved in
moved out again
I kept Farmlandia
going
over the years
skin plowed deep
too much sun on Irish
wrinkles to creases
flesh turned wilty
muscles into ache
breasts sagging
hips widening
I kept farming
I kept Farmlandia
going.

Over the years
Farmlandia suffered
bad weather
frosts and heat
rain and drought
hurricanes, hurricanes
1910, 1926, 1935
devastation all over
over and over, 1948
another due
any day, hurricane season
our annual ruination
Farmlandia suffered
bad turns
a killer flu
two world wars
economic slumps and pits
worse than the rutted road
from the coastline inland
to the farm
and over the years
Farmlandia lost everything
several times over—
the Depression especially
took a heavy toll
I kept the farm going
I kept Farmlandia.

Donal was here
Donal was there
Donal went overseas
Donal came back whole
Donal came back wounded
in his sweet soul.

Farmers farmed
farmers lost their land
Farmlandia hung on
with little to sell
just enough
for us
to survive.

Donal stayed in uniform
first as a warden
for Audubon
protecting plumed birds
from murderous plunder—
like our Papa had done
to feed us, his family
before populations waned
to near extinction
and the law stepped in.

Donal left the woods
for the US Postal Service
still in uniform
still happy
as a child he'd been
totally captivated
by the barefoot mailmen
who walked seventy miles
from Jupiter to Miami
crossing the inlets
in leaky old scows
back and forth
rain or shine heroes.

Donal loved the work
in shoes, no scows

a route near town
from the post office
in upscale Palm Beach
his daily jaunt
past thousands of coconut palms—
grown from coconuts
tossed overboard
when a ship ran aground
many years before—
green fronds swaying
in a lightly salted breeze
pretty as postcards
Palm Beach Donal
spending happy years
walking paved streets
and dirt back roads
talking, talking
to all the interesting men
making love to the women
drinking, drinking
with too many of them.

Out of money
still talking and drinking
he moved back home
to Farmlandia
with a too-young wife
expecting
his only child
after he lost
his mail carrier job.

He worked hard
when he worked
but took to alcohol

more readily
more steadily
he built
his own still
on the far backside
of Farmlandia
made his own whiskey—
a corn liquor
he aged
in charred oak
barrels—
sure had a bite to it
sold like mad
during Prohibition
shipped up the river
in tomato crates.

I took to it too
but only
on Saturday nights.

Over the years
Donal fell
under the influence
of his old wounds
his lack of parenting
his mistakes with women
his socializing
his drinking
and it ruined him
my little brother
a new father
a troubled man
he passed away
after a long wet spell

we buried him
beside Mama and Papa.

His wife Gina
pretty girl from the shacks
of West Palm
fled back to civilization
fled soon as he died
unhelpful to me
fighting with him
a disinterested mother
not a grieving widow
restless, black hair hived
above a lean sad face
one day
she was gone.

I was not surprised
farm life does not suit
most women, not
women like her
women in need
of the rapt attention
of men, parties and outings
but I was surprised
I was shocked
I was gladdened
beyond words
she left
she left Bibby
with me.

I'd watched that beautiful baby
sliding gracefully
into the old tin washtub

full of warm water
next to the woodstove
in my kitchen
little face pink
when they lifted her out
and I laughed
and I loved her
from that moment.

This was after
the last war
our luck changed
as luck does
over the years
we experienced grace
bountiful seasons
good crops
our simple kind
of daily gifts
farm wealth
a natural prosperity.

We ate well
Bibby happy
a happy baby
a happy child.

Over the years
I'd grown used
to having someone
in my wake:
first Donal
the cow dog Flora
my lame duck Peg
then Donal's daughter

his only child
Elizabeth
after our mother.

Always at my side
helping me
learning skills
she would need
in the future…
I was old
and getting older
sure I would
die
one day soon
enough
I would
leave her
behind
leave her
Farmlandia.

Every woman needs a future
she can count on.

At five Bibby took charge
of the chicken coop
by eight she was planting
and harvesting
like a hired man.
At nine she begged to learn
my treadle sewing machine
and became a talented quilter
by the time she turned ten—
one of her prettiest
made from Mama's old dresses

reminds me
of both Elizabeths.

She helped me
bake bread
cooking our meals
on the old stove
preserving the produce
making sour pickles
from garden cukes
heating up jars
of sweet berry jams.

She embroidered
fine stitched by hand
tiny colored flowers
on the one white tablecloth
beautifying
the dinner table
on Sundays.

She helped me
do the washing
on Saturdays
outside
in our ultra-modern
washer machine
gas-powered
with rollers
to squeeze out dirty water
the clothes and sheets
took us all morning
hands red and cramped
we hung it all
on the rope line

strung between palm trees
in the afternoon sun—
faster
than the ribbed washboard
when I used Octagon soap
at the creek, but
still slow
hard work.

She adopted
a blind white kitten
from a dead barn cat
bottle feeding him
raising him to follow
like a puppy
she loved Ghost
'til the day that poor cat
bumped into a plow blade
and went to the graves
under the big banyan.

Bibby made friends
with golden orb spiders
she called banana spiders
for their yellow hue
and played with the small
black beetles
until I told her
how they loved dung;
she chased butterflies
monarch and tiger-striped
letting them light
on her soft curls.

Over the years
Bibby and I
we grew
close, at night
reading together
by candlelight
on the porch
our battered
secondhand novels
White Fang
The Secret Garden
Little Women
the great poems
of the great poets
Carl Sandburg
Walt Whitman
Emily Dickinson
listening together
to the battery-powered radio
set on the woodstove—
when it ran out of juice
she'd scramble outside
to charge it up again
off the old truck battery.

Over the years
we relied on men
hired men
to help us
to gather the firewood
to repair the fencing
to cut acres of corn
to weed the bean fields
to harvest the citrus

from tall ladders
with their long, strong arms.

Over the years
we built a farm stand
and sold our produce
fresh and preserved
in pint, quart, and two-quart
glass Mason jars:
our jams and pickles
fresh picked corn
racks of fresh eggs
occasional baked goods
bouquets of wildflowers
the petals dazed
in the summer heat
like Bibby beside me
standing on a milking stool
counting out change.

Once a week
on Saturday afternoons
we took a drive
in the old truck
into town:
to drop off the corn
at the grist mill
to do some trading
at the grocery store
our eggs and chicken
for flour, sugar, sundries
and to the hardware store
for supplies
maybe sell a rooster
at the butcher shop

a cage of infertile hens
always a stop
at the diner
for a white bread sandwich
and a silver dish
of strawberry ice cream.

Every summer
we went to the beach
Palm Beach island
Bibby played in the waves
kickup and knockdown
her shoulders turning pink
mine a fiery red
we gathered pretty shells
and the big conch
we would pound and boil
into the thick chowder
we both loved.

Over the years
I bought her
so many things
a girl likes:
a white cotton dress
a forest green felt hat
a pair of shiny red shoes
I'd seen her looking at
in the Sears catalogue—
I had to order these things
through the mail
the stores in town
didn't carry much
for women and girls
a farm town

in a farm land
full of hardworking men.

She didn't seem to care
a happy child
in bare feet
and denim shorts.

When she was a toddler
Bibby wore bib overalls
and one of the hired men
told me one day,
You got to come out to the garage,
that little bibby gal
covered in axel grease.

Over the years
we looked at the sky
so many nights
before bed
Bibby and I
out front
stargazing,
diamonds glittering
on a black velvet cushion
like jewels in a pretty box
the size of heaven
our eyes upturned
to the swaying pines
waiting for the windy hoot
of the resident barn owls
to carry us inside
to our warm beds.

One hot summer day
the sky a bleached sheet
the air a wet blanket
the sun a red blister
Gina drove up
in a convertible Pontiac
her hair cut short
dyed yellow as corn
lips a blood streak
big mouth going, going
I couldn't fathom her
I didn't understand
why
she took my Bibby
with her
going, going
away
from me
from the farm
from Farmlandia.

To say I was inconsolable
would be a grave
understatement
to say she ruined Bibby
also understated
an impressionable child
dragged around
for five restless years
on the road rootless
as her damaged mother
a dust ball blown about

until one cold evening
after a long day

covering the citrus for frost
covering the garden for cold
covering myself with the quilt
made by my Bibby
I sat on the porch
legs up on the rail
warm in a wool jacket
lamb fur at my neck
cow dog Jack
by my side
a hot tumbler
in cupped hands
tea with a jigger:
coconut rum
freshly made
in Donal's old still
where I'd been brewing
cheap moonshine
with coconut water
and sugar syrup
from our cane field

and suddenly
I was surprised
I was shocked
I was gladdened
beyond words
beyond all measure
when my Bibby returned.

They pulled up
in a beat-up van
the unfamiliar driver
bearded, scowling
Gina beside him

beat-up, scowling
parked out front
beyond the gate
and from the back
out she popped—
tall, coltish
long pale legs
stringy hair
skinny and dirty

my Bibby
a teenager
a different child.

I took her in
my arms
I took her in
and bathed her
I took her in
and loved her
I'll always love her—
I still plan
to leave her
the land
the farm
Farmlandia.

The sun has set now
the farm dark
cool, quiet
the TV screen
of old memories
blank now
I will go inside
get in bed and read

Flannery O'Connor's
sad sad stories
until I fall asleep.
I must rise early
begin another day
all the chores
all the work
to keep Farmlandia
going.

The screen door creaks
when I open it
snap-bangs
when I let it close.

Over the years
I have learned
love and the land
are everything
in life—
everything
worth living for.

Conch Chowder

3 conch, shelled and prepared for cooking*
1 large onion, chopped
1 clove garlic, chopped
1 sweet pepper, diced
2 cups tomato sauce
1 lb. potatoes, diced
salt
pepper

1. Grind up prepared conch and set in a deep pot. Cover with water and boil for 30 minutes.
2. Add onion, garlic, sweet pepper; stir in tomato sauce.
3. Add potatoes, 3 cups of water, salt and pepper to taste.
4. Simmer until potatoes are cooked and fork tender.
5. Serve hot—makes enough for two.

*How to prepare conch:
1. Remove meat from shells and wash thoroughly.
2. Use a sharp knife to remove digestive end and thin covering; discard.
3. Soak conch meat in salted water for 2-3 hours.
4. Cut off any dark spots.
5. Pound with a mallet until smooth.

PART 4.

Elsa Ryan, Farmlandia, 1978

If I could rip out the concrete and put back the woods, I would. But I can't. Progress ain't reversible. What's done is done forever, and I'm sure as hell not proud of it. If any of you idiots had the brains of a jaybird you'd stop right now too.

—Patrick D. Smith, *A Land Remembered*

Each day gets more
difficult
to pull myself up and out
of this old sag bed
these old sag bones
full of ache.

I shouldn't complain
I have a full workload
and a body that can
still get up
and do it.

Coffee helps.
Coffee
always helped.

After a fifteen-mile trek
to the post, to Jupiter
to trade and barter
Papa would come home
the click of coffee beans
in burlap bags
he bartered for
at the settlement
purchased from a steamer
from the Indian River
Steamboat Company
the rich aroma
filling the little house
as he ground the beans
in Mama's flour grinder
as he boiled that coffee
on the cookstove

the smell so deep
so dark so intense
I felt it seep inside
my skin.

After he was gone
Donal and I
purchased beans
when the crops did well
we had plenty
of coffee
with our citrus groves
year after year
we had plenty
of everything
for a while.

Of course, later
we went without
for some years
before life changed
again and
Bibby and I
had coffee
year after year
until life turned
on us
again.

I rise slow
move slow
dress slow
out the bedroom window
the day lightens
the fickle sun

not high yet
but moving fast.

I brush out
my long gray hair
braid the thin strands
pin it up
thinking about
the work I must do
today
the work I do
every day.

The inside cats scatter
as I leave the bedroom
pad ahead
to find spoiled milk
in a forgotten bowl
trot to the barn
for handouts
from the kids who camp
on the farm.

The young folks tell me
they are here to help
but they are really here
for love,
free love—
as if there is
such a thing.

Love is not
free, love
will cost you—
sometimes

it costs you
everything.

In the sunny kitchen
I grind the beans
in a little grinder
boil the water
in a kettle
use the French press
to make
a big earthenware mug
of very strong coffee
so easy to brew
so easy now
so much easier now
on a modern-day farm.

How much has changed
over the decades
on the farm
and in Florida—
the population
booming
exploding
expanding
from just us few
hardy pioneers
to increasing hoards
newcomers, tourists
seasonal residents.

War brought them here—
which explains a lot
about the people
who live here now.

Three wars waged
against the Seminoles
in the 1800s
brought in cowboy troops
and support personnel
soldiers and supplies
needed to move fast
so the army built roads
and all the small settlements—
Fort Myers, Fort Meade
Fort Pierce, Fort Lauderdale—
became actual towns:
Fort Gatlin became Orlando
Fort Brooke, Tampa
Fort Dallas, Miami.

The Indian wars
led to more wars
led to the Civil War
the Spanish-American War
World War I,
each new conflict
bringing more soldiers
to Florida
to train and ship out,
and civilians followed
families and businesses
sprouting, taking root.
World War II brought
even more growth:
air stations and airfields
training centers and naval bases
millions of people

from every demographic group
entranced
by the topical beauty
that is floral Florida.
Many made the state
their permanent home:
a state of flowers
populated by wars
soldiers
conquerors
non-natives
outsiders.

In recent years
secret buyouts
thousands of acres
north of Farmlandia
trees and meadows
 and boggy soil
farmland to swampland
turning speculators and farmers
into instant millionaires
from the big build:
Disney's play city—
no respect for nature
will be its undoing
one day
long after
I am gone
a suburban wasteland
where everything looks
pristine, unused
lifeless
as a pretty postcard.

The developers keep on
developing
digging canals
sending brine water
to the ocean
where it doesn't belong
drying up the swampland
no longer fit
for habitat
for eagles and panthers
for bobcats and boar
for deer and bees and orchids
natural flora and fauna
dying slowly, dying off
the jungle staked out
for suburban sameness
for conquest, abuse.
My old Florida
a different world
a cool brand
a sunny place
for shady people
a busy place
honkytonk motels
dinky roadhouses
chicken dinner shacks
shops selling conch shells
glossed up with fake shine
goofy tee shirts
crates of oranges
a viral spread
of lookalike housing
asphalt to asphalt
development

edging ever closer
to Farmlandia.

I sip my coffee
bitter but good
sit down heavy
at the kitchen table
Frank made for me
from the cedar he cut down
that first year he was here
—after Donal left for the world
young and thrilled
before Donal returned from the world
still young but beaten down—
when I lived alone
when I lived with
Frank
only Frank
would make me
a gift
that would last
longer
than he did.

I savor bitter brew
allowing my thoughts
to float around
settle elsewhere—
in the near future
instead of the distant past
on chores to do
teenagers to check on
bills to pay
or shuffle
to the bottom

of the thick pile
of paperwork
best ignored.
My mind flurries
alights
flies off.
Despite such handicaps
due to my age I somehow
keep going, I've kept
Farmlandia
going
all these decades
somehow
I managed
through good times
and tough times.

Locals all around me
tired of scratching dirt
scratching out a living
captivated
enriched
by illegal activity:
imports from the South
freighters
carrying thousands
of pounds
of contraband
bales
hidden way out
in the Everglades
floating up on beaches
dropped from small planes
offloaded to outboards
shipped out to truckers

shipped north to users
blood on their hands.

I've kept mine clean
kept Farmlandia
going.

My mind flits over
the choices I've made
the coffee cold
in my worn hands
until I look up as

Billie appears
in the kitchen doorway
half-naked
long hair a thatched mass
blonde curls matted
to one side, greasy
knees black with dirt
the child
needs parenting
but when I try
to give it to her
she runs off
skittish and fleet
as a baby lamb.

Come sit, child,
I say, patting
the smooth tree trunk seat
beside mine
Frank made
these chairs
out of the same cedar trunk

smoothed them
with his big man's hands.
Sit, darling girl,
I'll make us
some sweet oats
with berries
and goat's milk.

She yawns
runs a dirty hand
though the mop of tangles.
I need to go for a swim,
Nonny, and clean up.

She canters through the room
across the porch
down the steps
through the tall grass
past the old barn
on a tilt,
past the garden
ripe and thrusting
she runs away
to the pond
long brown legs pumping
young body perfect
but her mind
not well—

she's been like this
wild like this
dirty like this
undisciplined, unearthed
since her mother left
Bibby left her behind

for a free life
for free love
with consequences
far away
in 'Frisco.

Bibby's child
Donal's granddaughter
crazy Billie
my responsibility
the girl
wild-eyed
confused
thinks I am
her grandmother
her *Nonny*
and I cannot
convince her
otherwise.

Fire's gone out
while I linger here
in a haze
of messy thoughts
I stand up
slow shuffle
to the potbellied stove
lift a black metal lid
from the firebox
to poke the chunks
of hardwood
light up kindling
a fire
will take a while
to get hot enough

to cook breakfast
meantime
I grind some corn
fresh picked
to make grits
then wander outside
to pick the new berries
I noticed yesterday
the wild haw
the air around them
vibrating, fizzing
with a honeyed buzz
bees and red berries
ripe enough
for eating.

On the front porch
on one of the old rockers
still in the still air
the pink- and blue-
stained all over
berry basket
sits and I am
waiting then
to catch my breath
my heart speeds up
slows
skips
speeds up—
something it's been doing
a little too often
a little too much
lately.

I gasp when
a man looms
but it's just the kid
Billie's beau
Dorgo
slips past me
barefoot
bare chested
in skimpy running shorts
not stopping to speak
not bothering to wave
like a wild animal too
his fervor
for my grandniece
like a rutting dog
following her scent
to the pond
to the city
for parties, drugs
whatever it is
they do together.

Teenagers
those two
no help to me
my only living relative
and her current mate
both close to the age
when I took over
Farmlandia,
how life has changed
during my lifetime.

Kids like Dorgo—

homeless
runaways
strangers
troubled teens
have been arriving
at Farmlandia
for years
in dribbles
in droves
attracted
to what's left
of wild Florida
to the primitive farm
the old way of life
on this fertile land
rich and real
they arrive alone
barefoot, dirty
in broken down Beetles
in curtained hippie vans
backpacks full of books
on organic farming
natural living
and tantric sex
and they beg me
to allow them
to help me
with the goats
the groves
the garden
the produce stand.

I'm grateful for the help
I'm an old woman
and the kids

so energetic
and enthusiastic
at first…

Excited to join in
they pitch their tents
in the cleared pasture
on the east side
of the land's edge
in a spot they call
The Camp
and sit around
smoke marijuana
cook over open fires
sing and drink
make love
jog to the pond
for cooling swims
hitchhike to the beach
the nightclubs
the cities
the kids all tell me
they want to
go back to the land
they want to live
the way I have
all these decades.

Do they really want
the lifelong responsibility
to keep a farm
like Farmlandia
keep it going?

The young girls
giggling, not shy
talk openly
about their dreams
to find the right man
to give birth in the fields
or under an orange tree
tucking new babies
in silky slings
to go back to work
they say
they want to feed
their families
only the food
they grow themselves
healthy produce
straight out
of organic gardens
fresh, clean
without chemicals
they tell me
they want to avoid
the miscarriages
their friends suffer
from pesticides
in the water supply
chemicals
in the food
these girls all claim
they want to milk
a sweet cow
and friendly goats
make their own cottage
cheese and yogurt
bake whole grain bread

weed and harvest
bottle and preserve
work, work, work
to survive.

But I know
what they really want
is to control their food
and control their farm
not let it
control them
I know
what they want
is not possible.

I can't say
I blame them
I can't argue:
a healthy farm
supports a healthy life
but truth is
our country
doesn't care
our small family farms
disappearing
all around us
due to
bad farm policy
from a government
hooked on supersizing
and overinvesting
in heavy equipment
expensive inputs
thousands upon thousands of acres
of wheat, corn, soy

making the kind of budget hole
nobody can crawl out from
big debt
for the row crop tractors
milking machines
animal medications
fertilizers, pesticides
for a food supply
now changed dramatically
lifeless and scraped
from depleted soil
thick with chemicals
lacking in nutrients.

When we first settled here
at Farmlandia
Papa added lime
to the sandy soil
to neutralize
the acidity
release the nitrogen
allow the growth
of healthy soil
bacteria
earthworms
zillions of microbes.

The birds and bees
loved it too
pollinators swarming
in a garden thick
with butterflies
the swallow tail kites
swirling overhead

when the slugging snails
needed culling.

And then Frank
convinced me
to compost
like my parents did
but I'd stopped
once county garbage trucks
began weekly pickups
way out here
at Farmlandia
Frank's composting
the garden soil turned
it deep black again
it's still black now
years later
rich in what's needed
what we all need
to be healthy.

The young folks love
to feed
the compost heap
behind the barn
food scraps
yard waste
weeds
husks
to help me
with chores
with the workload
the day's farming
energetic and enthusiastic
at first…

until
they pair up
make plans
drift off
break up
hurry back
to "real life"
or stay together
seek out
a homestead
their own plot
wherever they can
find land
that looks
unclaimed…

until
they get discovered
kicked off the land
because these days
all the land in Florida
is claimed land—
it wasn't always
this way,
Donal and I
were fortunate
to buy ours
when we did
just before the influx
of Northern speculators
developers scoping out
the Florida prairie
all that good cattle
grazing land

developers scooping up
the prairie
where previous speculators
had dug up
phosphate mines
and left
gaping holes
developers mapping out
blueprints and plots
for draining the swampland
for farmland and housing tracts
and beyond
west into the Everglades
all down the coastlines
out on barrier islands
taking it all
changing the landscape
forever.

Forced to claim
our parents' homestead
Donal and I
still young
still had savings
from our citrus groves
enough to pay for
all our land
our parents' land
five hundred acres
ours in deed
before the new wave
of real estate miners
moved in
transforming
this part of the world

into their own
private
goldmine.

I have no idea
what our land is worth
now
we only paid
pennies an acre
the land had long
paid for itself
no mortgage
required
through the rah-rah
1920s
the best of America
1940s
the new inventions:
cars
highways
electricity
refrigerators
mosquito repellant
replacing smudge pots
that didn't help
with advancements
that did
that made Florida
more accessible
that made Florida
more livable
a legible life
that made
the Florida land boom
that made values

skyrocket
that made Farmlandia
land rich
which lasted…

until
it didn't.

Frank was here
helping me
when we suffered
setbacks
back-to-back
freezes
took down
the citrus trees
ruined our produce
killed our chickens
our cows
almost killed me
sick with pneumonia
for weeks
Frank and I
scraping by
eating our own
homegrown
sweet potatoes
dug up
from the deep soil
baked or steamed
in stews and pies
sweet potatoes, sweet potatoes
so we could survive…

until
he didn't.

Frank died
in the cold
left me
alone
with the ruined groves
no food in the pantry
no money
no help
no man
I had to go to the bank
on my knees
beg to borrow
borrow to pay down
what I borrowed…

until
I built up
a mountain of debt
I can never pay off
will never pay off.

It's been years
since I lost Frank
more long hard years
of struggling
to survive
to keep going
to keep Farmlandia
to keep the land
going.

Male energy
is not always wanted
on a farm
testosterone
is not always good
on a farm
too many male animals
can cause injuries
fighting
unwanted breedings
and Frank
was like that too

but I allowed for that
I allowed for that
and we survived
and for a while
we thrived.

In the early days
of our acquaintance
much work was done
to improve the farm:
we painted the hardwood
exterior of the house
a bright white-
wash for the interior
updating the look
new furnishings
bigger windows
bigger doors
a tin roof
that sings in the rain
skylights
to brighten up rooms

we added a corn crib
a granary
a machine shed
for the single-share plow
and the cultivator
for weeding
and a rough-hewn garage
for the new Ford truck
we built a windmill
to draw the well water
a lot easier
on the arms
we added a water tank
in the barn
for the animals
our new system
filling the cistern
the water pumped
inside the house
running water
heated by the stove
for the first time ever
I washed dishes
in hot water
didn't have to bathe
in water boiled
on the woodstove—
the kind of stove
that requires a stove pipe
through the roof
so out of date

but I still love
and I still have
that simple stove

one change
I did not
want to make.

Frank had more ideas
on more modern
conveniences:
air-conditioned
cool instead of
fans or breezes,
in-house phones
instead of going to town
to the grocery store
to make our calls
Frank wanted lines
had them installed
all the way out
to the farm.

Frank said
the rest of America had
bathrooms
phones
electricity
commercially grown food
while I was still running
to the outhouse
other women
cooked on electric
or gas stoves the food
they took out of boxes and cans
while I braised
fresh-killed chicken
with just-pulled carrots
and just-dug potatoes

on the old woodstove
dumping potash
in the garden
so our food
had the smoked wood
flavor he liked
I liked
the old way
but he wanted
to make my life
easier.

He didn't understand
how much easier
it already was
with him there.

Frank bought the goats
told me how
after they give birth
you have milk for a year
delicious
easy to digest
goat's milk
the news spread
the community heard
the young mothers
coming by
buying our fresh milk
for their fussy babies.

We let the goats run free
inside the new fencing
Frank and I put up
they huddled in the barn

when the weather turned nasty
standoffish at first
nickering, nipping
if we got too close
their offspring friendly
the little ones
suckling our fingers
nuzzling our legs.

Those were good times
all that farm love
but I am old now
too old
to do all the milking
not brave enough
to cull
to kill for meat
my precious goats
I kill nothing
on this farm
no animals
no insects
no fungus
no inhabitants
of the soil
of the land
of Farmlandia.

Sometimes I think
I'd like to kill
the kids
these wandering teens
but they do help
but are unreliable
like Dorgo and Billie.

One of the young farmers
who got his start
here at Farmlandia
thanked me
with a pair
of puffy white sheep
the male a mean fellow
with a nasty bite
I didn't want them
I kept them
out of fear
of culling
of slaughter
for meat.

I'm not the girl
I once was
cutting off heads
of annoying chickens
carving up wild hogs
Papa shot
to cure for winter
I no longer eat
farm animals
deserve love and respect
I've come to believe.

The first year
the sheep mated
we added a single lamb
to the flock
and after that
litters of twins
I did not want to turn

Farmlandia
into a sheep farm
sold the small herd
to a neighbor.

Am I counting sheep?
My mind
has wandered
as I stand here
the sun hidden
but higher in the sky
abstract cloud art
draped in blue gauze.

In the shade
of the front porch
the day like a painting
the garden ahead
in reds and greens
bright orange, yellows
the purple of eggplant
the soil excellent
the goat manure
making it rich
with organic materials
the grove beyond
budded and full
the delicious aroma
of sweet orange
on a light easterly wind
the sun tucked away
but sure to burn hard
very soon
I must hurry
pick berries

eat breakfast
get going
on Farmlandia
keep going
on the full workload
of my busy day.

I push myself
through the sudden swarm
mewling barn cats
rubbing my ankles
with tawny fur
seeking milk
I tell them
Soon. Later.
I move quickly
as these old legs go
down the dirt path
past the tomato vines
the climbing beans
the low corn stalks
past the tin-roofed barn
where I hear the splat of milk
in steel pails
my teenage helpers
tending to goats
I rush by
not stopping
past the sauna
Frank's old cabin.

When Frank first came
to Farmlandia
before we were lovers
and slept in the same bed

he built himself
a little box
eight-by-eight
a handsaw and hammer
framed with cypress
pine board walls
a steel sink
and pipes
a pounded tin roof.

When he moved in
with me
he turned the cabin
into a sauna
told me all we needed now
was a salt water swimmin' pool.

Which made me laugh.

I smile now
but that passes
as I walk by the greenhouse
Frank built
before he succumbed
to the primitivism
we shared
pneumonia
I survived
on an old-fashioned farm
my farm
Farmlandia.

I still blame myself
I will always blame myself
for Frank's death

he lives now
in a little room
warmed by firelight
inside my heart
inside my mind
these days
he creeps out
many times
over and over.
When I arrive at the fences
that separate the goat pens
from the road
a hoot owl is waiting
black eyes in a mask
brilliant and knowing
silent, he lifts off.

I continue to wander
looking for the haw patch
crunching over striped snails
no forked-tail kites
circling overhead
the bees silent
the red hawberries
I can't find
I swear
they were here
plump, ripe
yesterday…

unless
that was *last* year
last summer?

I walk and walk
along the split-rail fence
Papa built.
Or Donal?
Frank?
Dorgo?

No, not Dorgo!
I laugh quietly
my mind
playing tricks
on me lately
I must be careful
to think clearly
but my knees
suddenly
buckle
and I lean
against the cypress fence
my pulse speeding
my heart stuttering
I drop
down, down
to a sitting position
my brain muddled
my body weakened
from something
I don't understand.

Or maybe I do:
after all
I have lived
I have survived
for all these decades
I am almost

a century old
and my life
has been nothing
but hard work—
plow
harrow
plant
cultivate
harvest
milk, muck, feed
water, graze, birth
dry, salt, freeze
bottle, preserve
heat and serve
package and sell
keep it going
keep going
Farmlandia.

I press a hand to my chest—
oh please
not here
not today
Billie's not ready
not yet
I still have
a dream
for her
for Farmlandia:
expand the farm
provide the community
with a whole food diet—
milk, cheese, butter
fresh eggs
whole grains

hand-picked fruits
and vegetables
so everyone
in our community
eats well
eats well from the land
our land
the land
we all share.

My heart races
as I picture the farm
Farmlandia
reborn:
a dozen Jersey cows
a brooder house for chickens
more goats, more goats
pigs roaming and rooting
in the soil
good soil
black and rich
with potash and manure
worms and microorganisms
new fencing
to protect the fields
and all the animals
from deer and bobcats
gators and panthers
a wide perimeter
of native trees
Florida spruce
scrub oak
to block the wind
keep the crops safe
delicious

nutritious
in demand.

In my mind
I am reading
a battered copy
of *Successful Farming*
ordering farm implements
for improvements
to achieve
what has been lost
to recapture
the fine art
of authentic farming
for a new state
of health
for the farm
for us
for the community.

In my mind
I am kneeling
on the floor
by the woodstove
the deep aroma
of fresh baked bread
in the warm room
one long braid bouncing
against my thin back
my hair shiny
and black
as crow feathers.

Wait:
is that me?

I feel myself
falling
falling
falling…

until
I am lying
flat against the soft ground
and I know
this is me
here
in the Florida dirt
and I know
I am old
I am going
I kept on going
I kept Farmlandia going
and I know this
truth:
a farm owns you
you do not own it
I married the land
I gave birth to it
this land my baby
my blood and flesh
and I hug it to me
and I merge with it
my land
my love.

My mind struggles
does not want
to let me go
not yet

I am not done yet
Papa told me
there is no such thing
as finishing work—
not on a farm.

I lie still
holding on
to my dreams
I feel ancient
like someone else's dream
from long ago
or the future
that has lodged
inside my head.

My mind slows
my pulse slows
I think how
nature persists
by consuming itself
on a farm
you cannot consume
more than you produce
so if I can no longer
work the land
I will let the land
take me
for its own use:
I will be
compost
for Farmlandia.

Nature is beautiful
and brutal I feel

my body trembling
my bones shaking
in the thin flesh cage
that holds me
here
my death a clarity
after years of struggle
trying to see clearly
until

Frank
is standing over me
muscled arms outstretched
his face handsome
as the day I first saw him
hat in hands
asking me
for work.
He is reaching out to me
those big strong hands
and I take them
in mine
his fingernails dirty
black soil caked underneath
our soil
good
healthy
Florida soil
the rich dark soil
that allowed us
to grow our food
to survive
and thrive.

Sweet Potato Pone

2 sweet potatoes
½ cup sugar
4 tbsp. butter
½ tsp. salt
2 eggs, beaten
1 cup milk
½ tsp. cinnamon
½ tsp. nutmeg

1. Peel sweet potatoes. Add to a pot of boiling water.
2. Boil until fork tender; drain, mash until smooth.
3. Add rest of ingredients and stir, mixing well.
4. Place in a buttered baking dish, and bake in a hot oven for 1½ hours.

PART 5.

Billie Ryan, Farmlandia, 1995

*But...ye shall destroy their altars, and break down
their images, and cut down their groves...*
                              —Deuteronomy 7:5

*One of the penalties of an ecological education
is that one lives alone in a world of wounds.*
                              —Aldo Leopold

The thing is,
you know almost nothing
about Billie Ryan
but you probably know
about where she worked:
Tybald Farms
where your corn comes from
where Florida corn is grown
shipped everywhere
made into everything
you eat from a box
a can
a Styrofoam clam.
As you probably know,
Tybald Farms means corn
tall as a barn
sweet as sugarcane
acres and acres
the biggest ears
the goldest corn
the most popular
best priced
corn
in the county.
Billie ought to know
she farmed some
of them acres
acres and acres
for a decade—
this was after
she inherited the farm
she inherited the debt
after Nonny died
Billie still living
in Nonny's old place

the sagging floorboards
the sloping walls
the potbellied stove
the humid rot
in every room.

Billie and Dorgo
they worked the farm
they changed the farm
to a single crop farm—
corn
easy to grow corn
easy to sell corn
and they survived
for a while.

Thing is,
back in the old days
Nonny said
backs bent, feet sore
you'd pick ripe corn
for days
by hand
spread the cobs
on the floor
of the barn
to dry, then husk
by hand
one cob at a time
before running 'em through
a hand-turned
sheller
everything by hand
even if the corn
got moldy

you'd grind it
for animal feed,
and if it was good
you'd sell it—
a lot of work
by hand
for a lot less corn
than is produced
by Tybald Farms.

But that's the way it was and
Billie's ancestors (some of them)
worked the fields
corn and other crops
human-drawn single plows
calloused bodies
fourteen-, fifteen-hour days
sunup to sundown
working
the farm
the way Nonny did
her whole long life.

Not Billie, not her
the modern farmer
bought a tractor
bought a big machine
that pulled the plow
the disk
the sprayer and spreader
the cultivator
worked the soil
with them machines
made the cornfields

produce, produce
and boy did she
show way more
crop productivity
than Nonny
and her parents
before her
could ever imagine
'cuz Billie
the modern farmer
stayed focused
on a single crop:
corn.

She sat up there
high up there
in the driver's seat
and made that corn
grow, grow, grow!

No garden beans
no tomatoes
no squash
no melon
no greens
no cukes
no sweet potatoes
no berries
no pineapple
no orchards
no citrus trees —
no oranges
no lemons
no grapefruit
no limes

no tropical trees—
no guava
no mango
no papaya
no avocado and
no more hay to mow
no animals to feed
no cows
no goats
no chickens
no fresh eggs
no milk
no butter to churn
nothing to preserve
nothing to cook
nothing
but
corn.

Billie and Dorgo
bare feet up
loungin' on the porch
after work
whistles wet
catchin' a buzz
watching money grow
out there
in the cornfields
acres and acres
of gold and green
corn, corn, corn
far as the eye could see.

Billie the modern
industrialized farmer

thought they had it all
so savvy
so up-to-date
smarter than all them
who came before
better than all them
who built everything
by hand
everything she had
ever been given
on this farm
in this life.

Thing is,
Billie knew nothing—
ignorant
foolish
a sucker
she worked the soil
worked with fertilizers
worked with pesticides
breathed the dust
it got on her clothes
it got in her hair
in her eyes
in her lungs
in the pores of her skin
she was soaking in it
for years and years.

Billie and Dorgo
worked pretty hard
played pretty hard
sold their homegrown
to other local players

Billie and Dorgo
started up the still
in the sinkhole
cooking up moonshine
old-style
extra-proof
kick-ass whiskey
with added capacity
to suit their needs
their customer base
for low bush 'shine
two bucks a pint
from the eighty-gallon still
pumping day and night.

Billie and Dorgo
they did okay
they were making it
they had them their fun
they had them their times
they didn't know nothing
about what they didn't know:
the water was tainted
the land, the air
their bodies
absorbing poisons
into blood
into organs
into cells
and DNA
which explains all them
miscarriages
too many
to cry about

and all them illnesses—
rashes, allergies, coughs
lungs full of fluid
different kinds of infections
sleep problems, mental
stress and all that
they treated with pot
their potent moonshine
kept on growing
corn, corn, corn.

The thing is,
the Big C:
for years and years
C was for corn,
now C's for cancer
and cancer is
forever.

Billie was surprised
herself
to find herself
wearing out her life
like an old housedress
the laundry smell of phosphates
rising from her pores
her featherless body
a crushed bird
broken and disjointed
whitewashed, skinned alive
not working
not partying
lying flat
in a hospital bed
oxygen mask

on her sallow face
flesh abandoned
in a sorry heap
of porous bones
lying in wait
for the call.

The call to go
meet her Maker.

Billie being one
of the many casualties
of the Green Revolution
and its greedy viral spread
the Green Revolution being
the trick name
for when the chemical industry
started converting war poisons
into crop pesticides
and convinced the world's farmers
to use them
to grow just one thing
acres and acres
of just one crop
per farm.

The chemical company pitch:
more inputs equals
more product equals
more money
for less work
for farmers.

You don't know much
about Billie

because you don't know
about the near future
when people like her
modern farmers
and their poor families
and their unlucky neighbors
will number
in the millions,
so many of them
you can't ignore them
growing silently
like the cancer cells
killing them
and soon enough
they'll be screaming
in your ears
with the pain
of their affliction
the pain
of our ignorance
of all we've lost
from illness and death
destruction and ruination
the bone piles
mounting slowly
not yet visible
not yet
not until
the day someone starts
adding them up
the day data scientists
begin doing the math.

Math is what got to them
math is what'll take them
someplace else
someplace healthy
and safe
a place where everyone
can live well
eat well
live right
in nature
the way Billie's Nonny
the way her ancestors
once lived.

Thing is,
that day
is too far
in the future
for Billie—
just another woman
in a hospital bed
in crisp white sheets
in her living room
the room she grew up in
playing by the woodstove
while Nonny made a snack
sweet jam on fresh bread
homemade citrus marmalade
slathered
on a thick slice
of wheat toast
a glass of fresh goat's milk
Billie and Nonny
seated on the plaid couch
with the springs poking out.

That broke old couch
still in the living room
thing is,
it ain't a living room now
it's a dying room.

Billie is laid out
like a shrinking pile
of rotting compost
squalid, squandered
on sweat-soaked sheets
looking back
in flashes of immense
breathtaking beauty
looking down
from a veiled distance
at her discarded carapace
cracked open, raw
undergoing its cycles
of fever spikes
alternating chills
the shaking
the drifting
she knows herself
knows what she is
craving
lying in wait
for one more
high
lying there lusting
for the goodbye rush.

Dorgo's out now

scavenging
his cruelties apparent
even to strangers
he begs and barters
for Billie's final need.

You might think
that's what's killing her
but you'd be wrong.
The farm is killing her:
Farmlandia.

The smell of phosphorus
from rampant fertilizers
the sweet reek of burning
from charred fields
water that tastes blued
a loitering taint
the choking smog
of a ransacked land
she feels ashamed
she had forgotten
to take care
of the land.

When you grow up
on a farm
you learn to take care
of the land
you learn to love it
tropical not tamed
half-wild you learn
about life
early
you know about animals

the birds and bees
the cows and goats
wild pigs and horses
you know about work
how to ride a row tractor
right
so you can see all them
plantings
how to hitch the drag
to comb the soil
and spread them seeds
how to hay up
anything green—
alfalfa, clover, grass
and you can sure tell
the difference
between hay and straw
you can make windrows
use a baler
you know how
hay can catch fire
if it gets too moldy
you know how
a ruminator eats
how to feed
its four special stomachs—
the first one for fermentation
then the regurgitation
the chewing
the cud—
you never give them
new foods
or if you do
then you do it
real slow.

You can make pickles
real fast
two weeks
in a crock
a layer of garlic and dill
fresh cukes you just picked
and brine
you know how
to spread seaweed
over the fields
in the down months
you know how
to butcher a chicken
repair fences
midwife the newborns—
all types.

Where there's livestock,
there's also dead stock.
Dead animals and
dead people
don't frighten you
when you grow up
on a farm
you see death
your whole life
on a farm
you know to use up
all of the dead
animals
no waste—
life goes on
and you
don't
waste

any of it.

Thing is,
when you grow up
on a farm
you think you know
how life works:
it works like it does
on the farm…

until
you get sick
with cancer
the farm sick
with misuse
the animals sick
the crows falling
from hidden perches
the European starlings
silent, still
piles of dead birds
like the black pyres
for an ancient ritual
to the corn god
the cancer god.

Growing corn
at Farmlandia
for Tybald Farms—
a subsidiary
of Tybald International
Corporation—
Billie and Dorgo
worked the land
like indentured slaves

they worked for a cut
of their own corn
sales
for a faceless company
with rules
for growing:
years
of poisonous pesticides
years
of polluting fertilizers
years
of nothing but corn
not growing their own food
buying meals from stores
in packages and cans
years
of doing every day
what they were contracted
to do
to apply
to the crops
to the land
air
water
toxins
poisons
that ruined
air
land
water
for miles around
and them
rented out
to the corporation
they had no say

immersed
in poisonous farm aids
a poisoned well
their poisoned lives.

Tybald
caused the cancer
which is robbing Billie
of her future
a large family
all the babies
never born
except
by early grace
her only child
before Tybald
caused the cancer
which robbed Billie
of her womb.

Thing is, you'll see
soon enough
the coming avalanche
of lawsuits
against the big companies
medical experts testifying
sad families shaking fingers
at corporate executives
in thousand dollar suits
you will see coming
state by state bans
on the toxic chemicals
a gradual turning away
of farmers
a turning back

to the old ways
of growing food
the old ways
of farming
of eating
the old ways
Billie's Nonny
and her ancestors
relied upon
for generations
the old ways that respect
soil
air
water
health
animals
people
land.

Nonny lived to a hundred
out in the hot sun
out in the cool rain
out in the gardens planting
weeding, harvesting
back bent, feet sore
under soft white clouds
like a pillow overhead
gray thunderclouds
marching to victory
lightning flares held high
whatever Florida gave her
Nonny worked on
always on her own
always doing chores
every day she lived

nearly triple the number
in Billie's foreshortened life.

While Nonny looked down
at the black soil beneath her boots
looked up and out
at orange sunrises, citrus trees
green gardens and groves
ripe produce, grazing animals
birds and insects and wildlife
her world a humming hive
she looked out for all
she lived for, loved
tending to the harvests
tending to the orchards
tending the land
for almost a century
she missed the worst
development, destruction
multinationals, bulldozers
horizons razed and rubbled
old trees into wood chips
her land into stripped plots
of corn, corn, corn
all around her land
mono-farms of soy, sugar, corn
dramatic changes that took over
the land, the land she loved
and her fellow farmers
sold out, worn out, dead.

While Billie lies inside
looking out, gazing
wistful and drifting
clouds a polka-dot smatter

in a dark blue sky
the smell of rain
ahead of itself
a languid emptiness
fills her like a high
she knows
she's wasted
years, everything
her bones yellow
crumbling
pallid organs
shutting down
skin a parchment
bald scalp
blued and shiny
pretty curls
long gone
her brain flickers
her conscious mind
floats up
on the ceiling
looking down
at what's left
of her:
a sad pile
of gray ash.

Billie turns her head
gazes out the window
at the sagging porch
the sandy dirt land
and after that nothing
but cornfields
lurking all around, inching
toward the house, covering

the land, what's left of the land
where citrus groves once flourished
where gardens once grew
the sweet pond filled in
years ago
with corn, corn, corn
the many acres
acres and acres
of Tybald corn
sucked up all the water
all the way to the ocean
no wonder
no birds chirp
in the few spindly trees
no bees swarm
no butterflies either
no cricket sounds
no sparks of fireflies
to light up the dark
no owls hooting
no animals howling
in the night
quiet, quiet
but for the rustling
of green stalks
those barren husks
bred in a distant laboratory
from poisons and greed.

Billie stares out
the dusty window
and corn
corn
corn is all she sees
even when she closes her eyes

she can see only
corn
nothing
but acres
and acres
of stiff yellow corn
row after row
of corn soldiers
a vast army
of deadly corn
when she looks out
the window now
Billie sees
her own
murderer.

Thing is,
all she wants now
is to get high
float up to the ceiling
and out the window
keep floating
over the fields
past all the acres
far away from there
away from the corn
away from the land
that surrounds her
that holds her prisoner
land she never
loved
land
abandoned, abused
it turned on her.

Fierce, this land
Florida
Farmlandia
is fierce.

The land was harsh
before it was conquered
and harvested
respectfully, solicitously
by Billie's ancestors
the land now
a factory
forced to produce
against its own nature
beaten up
brutalized
and turned
deadly
the killer soil
toxic
to all life.

The sandy soil
so carefully enriched
and maintained
and revered
by Billie's ancestors
now
lifeless:
it takes away
life
no longer gives it.

Farmlandia and Billie
surrounded by

lifeless dirt,
dirt as lifeless
as they are.

When the phone rings
her bony hand crawls
across damp sheets
like a land crab.

Digger lifts his head
from his black paws
sets his white muzzle
on the bed, sniffs
at her veiny hand
until she pets him
she loves
that old dog
her personal bodyguard
he watches Dorgo carefully
with hooded eyes
but Dorgo never
hits her
not anymore
Billie would break
if he touched her
she would explode
into fragments
sift down
upon the land
a smattering
of used-up
dust.

She answers the phone
the line quiet

she says, *Yeah?*
hoping
it's not
the electric company
the bank
the doctor's office
regarding
the unpaid bills
the last ten months
and the months before.

Mommy, it's me,
a small voice says.

Donald
her boy
her little man.

Billie's shell softens
her heart beats rapidly
in her hollow chest
her baby
so far away
she coos, *Hi, honey.*
You having fun
with your cousins?

Billie aches
to hold
her boy
her baby
her Donny
one more time
take him to Disney
walk the crowded park

see the wonder and joy
in her little boy's eyes
but she won't
let him see her
not like this, no
he can never see her
this way
this sick
this gone.

*We went to a movie
about a karate kid.
I want to learn
karate, Mommy.*

She won't leave
her baby boy
with Dorgo
Billie loves Dorgo
but being with Dorgo
guarantees
failure.

*Of course you do, baby.
Ask Aunt Karen
to sign you up
they have
classes like that
they have
everything
up there
in Jacksonville.*

She has plans

for the future
for Donald's care
a standing offer
from Tybald
and at this point
the end point
for Billie
she plans to take it
leave
all the cash
for Donny's care
this is her will—
what's left
of Farmlandia
the rest of the acres
they did not sell
they did not farm
they left fallow
she will sell now
to Tybald—
but they won't get
the very last acre
or the house
Nonny's house
what's left of
the old home
the heart of
Farmlandia.

Donny chatters
in his baby voice
Billie dozes
'til he runs out
of little boy stories

she wakens
to tell him
I love you
more than the world
and over the moon
and he giggles
says *bye*
and she fades
drops the phone
misses the cradle
misses Digger
misses her baby
her boy
her little man
her mind
adrift
floats
across the fields
of corn
corn
more corn
acres and acres
of genetically modified
sprayed and neutered
monocropped corn.

Would Billie have sold off
bit by bit
over the years
acre upon acre
so much of the land
so much of Farmlandia
sold out
to Tybald
had she known

back then
what that would do:
to Farmlandia?
to the community?
to all of you?

Yes:
because
she had no choice
the debt from Nonny
the debt she accrued
more debt piling up
from mortgages
equity loans
equipment loans
money running out
their farming skills
too poor
to keep the farm
to keep Farmlandia
going.

Billie wasn't 100%
clean and clear
when she signed over
much of the deed
for Farmlandia
acres upon acres
gone
and soon enough
Billie will sign over
most of what's left
the bill of sale
her own last
will and testament.

Thing is,
she was not the only one
around the county
who gave up
the family farm
once farm kids
left to carry on
the family business
failed—
most of them
better farmers
than Billie and Dorgo
real farmers
who worked the land
desperately trying
to pay mortgages
with falling crop prices
diminished fertility
always the next level
of reduced productivity
the crushing pressure
of potential foreclosure
so many succumbed
sold out
to corporate entities—
they all felt
they had
no choice.

Thing is,
you
have no choice now
because of this
because of food companies

because of agriculture companies
because Big Food, Big Ag
because small farmers
sold off
your food basket.

When Billie signed over
the orchards
the gardens
the trees and wildlife
all that good land
most of Farmlandia
died
and she gave up
your good food
your good health
your good future
she thinks now
in her living room
in her dying room
on her deathbed
she is so sorry
sorry
sorry
sorry
for Billie
for Donny
for the community
for you
your future.

Thing is
you'll see one day
after you are no longer
swimming in the sweet green

of better days
you'll understand why
poor Billie
was dead
wrong
but please
don't blame her—
remember what she realized
too late
how she lost
everything
too.

Hoe Johnny

1 cup cornmeal, stoneground
½ tsp. salt
hot water
fat (lard or butter)

1. Combine cornmeal with salt.
2. Add enough hot water to make a stiff batter.
3. Drop by large spoonfuls in hot fat.
4. Fry thick cakes until brown.
5. Turn over; fry other side until brown and serve hot.

PART 6.

Valeria Morales, Farmlandia, 2020

*If we are the greatest nation the sun ever shone upon,
it would seem to be mainly because we have been able
to goad our wage-earners to this pitch of frenzy.*
—Upton Sinclair, *The Jungle*

The room dark, hot
as usual
in this tin can
I arise in a sweat
get ready to go
to work.

On my own today
as usual
the only one
heading to the factory
Mom not working
Donny staying home
sick
I tiptoe around
the trailer
wash up, dress
make a thermos
of milky Mexican coffee
in the little kitchen
that smells like swamp cabbage
from last night's dinner.

Through paper-thin walls
Donny coughs, coughs
my mother murmurs
soothing, soothing
his nurse
his savior.

Alone this morning
in the Florida heat
I sit on the front stoop

pull on my workboots
in the morning blueness
sip my café
look at the night sky
the almost-morning sky
beyond the empty fields
a hangnail moon
like a shimmer of cream
slick and cool
pouring down
lightening up
my dark forearms
my small hands
to a pale wash.

My imagination
gets me through
long dull days
at the factory
just to the west.

In the gradual light
I walk slow
down the road
my feet heavy
on asphalt
clunk clunk
heavy boots
necessary
on the factory floor
clunk clunk
on hot asphalt,
the same asphalt
that covers the land,
barren land

hot, sandy, treeless
sad land.

A mile to go and
I already smell
the ammonia
the chicken reek
when the wind blows east
the stink
so strong
my eyes burn
at home
in Donny's trailer
my head aches
my sinuses blocked
my throat a scrape
the horrible stench
after work
my clothes
my hair
my skin
fetid odor
of chicken blood
chicken guts
chicken shit
after a shower
lots of soap
scented shampoo
I still smell
chickens!

No way
to get rid of it
no way
for me

to smell
nice
like a normal
teenage
girl.

Thank god
I'll be back
in school
in the fall
thank god
I'm only working
at the factory
for now
while schools
in Florida
are closed.

Kids call it
plague-cation
for me a stay-
working-cation.

Clunk clunk
past shuttered farmhouses
boarded up windows
rusted automatic feeding machines
skeletons of tractors
machinery carcasses
collapsed barns
rotten bank loans
credit union loans
government bailouts
nobody could afford
to work the land

themselves
all cogs
in one giant supply chain
a global chain
choking us
to death.
Grim thoughts!

I stop to open
the thermos
slug warm coffee
check the sky
for stars
the moon
still there
a bright sickle
above my head.

I'm working doubles
all week
they need the help
so many workers out
sick
we need the cash
I used to work
school vacations
not full time
not doubles
not for long
I'm a junior
at Tybald High
my grades
good enough
for college
I'm on debate team

assistant editor
our yearbook
founder and president
our school Climate Club
from a distance
you might think
you're looking at
a normal
teenage
girl—
but you'd be wrong
that's not
who I am.

Up close
I smell bad
fingernails cracked
hair slimed
with the gross grease
of animal offal
so disgusting
so repulsive
I hate myself
I'm a loser
like my mom.

She was doing okay
for a while
working days
at a nursery
selling pretty palm trees
and bright flora
for landscaping
after Dad split
it was hard

but we coped
a good team
always home
for dinner
together.

But then she met him
Donny:
sweet
handsome
fucked up
Donny
the druggie parents
the sold-off family farm
the generations of bad luck
and of course
big-hearted Mom
fell for
his personality
his boyish charm
his sexy badboy allure
and we moved here
to what's left
of his family's land.

Then it got worse
she quit her job
to make house
for the guy
like some '50s
housewife
in a sitcom fantasy world
which lasted months
a kind of love bliss
I couldn't stand

to watch
I was glad
so glad
for school.

One day
my dear mother
came out of her trance
finally noticed
Farmlandia
the once famous hippie farm
with a legendary past
was in terrible shape
all weeds, no crops
no fresh food
on our table
the garden shot
the animals gone
the cornfields destroyed
the soil trashed
nothing could grow
not even corn
the air and water
the land itself
reeking
from the chicken factory
up the road.

Donny the owner
of the very last acre
of his family farm
with a rusty trailer
the old farmhouse
trashed in a hurricane
in 2005

that tumbledown house
his parents once lived in
and his great grand aunt
a kooky old lady
who spent a hundred years
in a house built
in the 1800s
by *her* parents
all the way back
in the cowboy days
a whole lineup
of Florida crackers
living and dying
in that old house.

I love it,
what a story
so historic.

The lightning jags
and thunder booms
out of a bluing sky
out of nowhere
and I speed up
coffee dregs sloshing
around the thermos
I am of the opinion
that old house
should be saved
artfully
rehabbed
but Donny
hasn't got the money
he boarded it up
to protect it

from critters
teenagers
squatters
thank god
he's sentimental
you wouldn't think it
to look at him
but he has heart.

Mom was the first
of us
to land a job
at Tybald Poultry
the salary so low
she couldn't keep us
afloat
so after some
needling
cajoling
love talk
Donny took a job too
at Tybald Poultry.

Then I volunteered
to work on occasion
on school breaks
I'm that kind of girl
but now I regret it
the dead chicken
stink
could ruin
the rest of
my life—
if the job

doesn't
kill me
first.

Still no rain
just bouts of thunder
and zigs of lightning
in the distance
Florida dry
so dry
all the time
not much swamp
mostly brush
and dead fields.

I stop
just short
of the guard gate
light up
a Marlboro
stand there
smoke it down
to the filter
crush and slip it
back in the pack
and listen
and tip my head
in wonder
when I hear
a faint
hoot
and an owl
an owl!
swoops down
lands on the asphalt

on the asphalt!
sits motionless
staring at me
at me!
then flies up again
into brightening sky.

I am so shocked
I cannot move
for a minute
a whisper of joy
wrapping around me
I never see
wildlife
birds
bugs
animals
except rats
and roaches
I'm thrilled
and laughing
and my mood
lifts.

I gather myself
strap on my mask
a quilted piece
I made myself
from Donny's old shirts
and approach the guard gate
get out my badge
go through security
get scanned
mentally undressed

by fat dudes in uniform
I ignore and hurry off
down the asphalt walkway
to the employee entrance
my mood sinking
with the usual
boredom
disgust
apprehension
hatred
for all things chicken.

I spray breath mint
under my mask
listening to
the warehouse echo
with my work mates'
chatter and
hack, hack.

Since Donny tested positive
Mom can't go to work
he's not getting better
and it's been weeks
it's weird to see him
lying on their bed
in his underwear
all day
not dancing with her
in the tight kitchen
not riding his old Harley
to Jimmo's
sports bar
where he hangs out
where he caught

covid
he thinks
but I doubt it
so many workers
at the factory
have coughs
that sound
exactly like
Donny:
hack, hack.

I shouldn't be working
living with covid
I could be
asymptomatic
like many young people
but someone has to
work
we need to eat
pay the bills
overdue and
all Tybald employees
got a two dollar
an hour
plague raise
that won't last
I have to
take advantage
now and guard
my anonymity
at the factory
my manager
doesn't know
I live with Donny
I'm just one

of many
brown faces
on the line
my coworkers
know nothing
about me
they couldn't care
less, I'm young
younger than them
I don't talk much
most of them
don't speak
much English
I keep my head down
and focus
on the line.

I used to work
on grading,
arranging
soggy white breasts
thighs and legs
in orderly piles
on the belt
the raw meat
headed for packaging
mindless
but not dangerous
work
but now they move us
around
to different stations
every day
depending on
who's absent

I take on shifts
come home tired
soak swollen hands
in hot water
especially after I'm on
the cut up line
plucking small bones
fast as I can
makes me tired
fingers sore
just thinking about it.

I keep moving
enter the locker room
with the rest
the morning shift—
nobody takes our temperature
warns us
to keep social distance
or tests us
for covid.
Tybald don't care
as long as the floorwork
gets done
as long as you pull count
as long as the conveyor belt
keeps moving.

Keep the belt moving!
at any cost.

I go to my locker
where some of the workers
hang out, chat, cough
I am silent

my breath
trapped in my mask
smelling of smoke
coffee
minty
chicken.
I dress
in protective wear:
coveralls
goggles
gloves
hairnet
hard hat
foam ear plugs
handmade mask.

We file out the door
to the hallway
wait
in a long line
for our turn
to punch in
some wearing masks
some not
standing around, shifting
crammed together
bodies close
enough
to smell one another's
old sweat, soap
deodorant—
this embarrasses me
more than anything
about this job

I don't want anyone
to smell me.

When it's my turn
I grab the time card
that says
Valeria Morales
clock in
then walk to the offices
looking for my manager
I need a medical mask
I could be carrying
the virus
I could be
a super spreader
I don't want to be
Typhoid Mary
at Tybald Poultry.

I don't see my manager
anywhere
I head back
to the air-locked
double door
everyone else
on morning shift
lining up too
ready to face
another day
on the belts
long lines of belts
the belts all moving—
all day and all night.

Up we go
onto the catwalk
above harvesting
the kill floor
the earsplitting din
of factory machinery
fills my head
like a punishment
the stink of blood
mixed with poop
mixed with ammonia
chlorine bleach
makes me swoon.

Bones cold, breath held
I cross the catwalk
above the slaughter
the chickens on the belt
hung by yellow feet
quick slice of the carotid
still twitching, alive
entering the tunnel
to be spray-washed
defeathered by machine
rebranded *white meat.*

In the packing room
I descend quickly
to my assigned position
on the fabrication floor
scan the room
for my manager
the lines
tight today
the workers

sore shoulder to shoulder
some gaps
where employees
missing
some people
working two belts
a huge challenge
since the lines move
at different speeds
fast
or faster
than they used to
due to recent changes
in regulations
the President
wanting us to produce
more *white meat*
faster and faster
for hungry homebound
Americans—
which sounds patriotic
until you learn
most of the chicken
packaged here
is shipped
to China.

The line buzzer goes
I step into position
as the short, squat woman
on night shift
nods at me
moves off.

I think the line moves
way too fast now
us line workers
are afraid
we'll get hurt
like last week
when an old man
lost a thumb
in evisceration
my manager said
it was his own fault
he wasn't paying attention
he'd been taking on
too many doubles
too many shifts
in a row
for a guy
over sixty-five.

The chain must go on
management says
the belt never stops
no matter what.

Donny's friend
from the sports bar
worked at Tybald
until
both hands got
crushed
in a hammer mill
and before he got sent
to the emergency room
his manager made him
sign a waiver

of responsibility
with a pen
held
in his teeth.

My manager
nowhere in sight
maybe she's out
sick
I scan
my coworkers:
the slumped shoulders
the red-rimmed eyes
the downcast faces
the bloated bellies
the bloodied coveralls
everyone looks
exhausted
scared
beyond hope
yet none of us
slack
we all pull count
work the line together
keep the belt moving.

When the line buzzer goes
my hands are ready
to move
fast
faster, faster
the tickle in my throat
making me
want to
cough.

Swamp Cabbage

white bacon or salt pork
2 heads swamp cabbage
sugar syrup
salt
pepper

1. Fry up the fat and set aside.
2. Chop swamp cabbage and put in a large pot.
3. Add hot fat, a dollop of sugar syrup, and enough water to fill
the pot halfway.
4. Bring to a boil; boil for 10-15 minutes or until cabbage is fork
tender.
5. Drain; add salt and pepper to taste.

Swamp cabbage is the heart of the cabbage palm tree and removal
kills the tree; best to substitute 2 cans of hearts of palm.

EPILOGUE

Valeria Morales, Farmlandia, 2038

Loneliness…
permeates the farmyard
and the farmhouse,
it sits
in front of the television in the
evening
drinking
a single cup of coffee.
—Knut Sørensen, *Farming Dreams*

In the cool sweet air
of early morning
the crickets chirp
then calm
as the sun rises
in a cloud soft sky
heating up
a tropical variation
on autumn
all around me
brilliant colors—
emerald and teal
reds, oranges
pinks and purples
gold, peach, *blue!*
a garden bounty
a luminescent continuum
I have grown
on my own.

Before dawn
I milked the goats
filled their wood troughs
with ground up
corn and oats
fed the greedy sow
mucked out the stalls
sniffed my clothing:
I smelled
like manure
so I went back inside
Donny's old trailer
for a shower
a change

into clean shorts
a fresh tee
and now I smell
better
thank god
I smell like
a normal
woman.

Above me
white herons slice sky
the fat clouds backlit
by the glowing orb
of a voluptuous sun
and nature, as always
keeps going
doing whatever it likes.

Flora trots beside me
licks my hand
as we wander around
the vegetable garden
my faithful mutt
she thinks she's guarding
me
I guess—
but from what?
There's nobody around
for miles
and miles
I've looked
and it's just me
the farm
and my dog—
not sure where

she came from
just showed up
one rainy day
skinny
mangy
bug-eyed
friendly
I fed her
cold carrot stew.

I fell in love
with the old dog
named her
Flora, like the state
the wild plant life
on this old farm:
Farmlandia.

The pandemics
the storms
the hurricanes
the floods
sea level rise
did a number
on the coastlines
on the county
on the state
Florida
killed off
residents
rich land
paradise lost
I lost everyone
close to me
the area lost

our main source
of employment
Tybald Poultry
shut down
fled
back to China.

After the chicken smell
finally faded
this area
still deserted
forlorn
a cemetery
of the defeated
the jobs did not return
the people did not return
by that time
I hadn't worked
a shift
in years
spending
a long time
caring for Donny
after my mom
got too sick
she died.

I never did save enough
money to attend college
but with nothing to do
I took some free
online courses:
environmental science
regenerative agriculture
how to make land

healthy
prosperous.

That kind of knowledge
comes in handy
when you're alone
on what used to be
a farm
on what could be
a farm
again.

The five hundred acres
where the factory once stood
abandoned
overgrown
not mine
per se…
I mean
I didn't buy it
but nobody
stepped up
nobody else
wanted it
and I'm here
so I'm homesteading
most of those acres
of abandoned Florida
land.

I hand-sow seeds
green shoots pop up
overnight
my plants
grow

big
fast
after the harvest
I save some seeds
to hand-sow
the next year
taking advantage
of the land
I live on:
diversity
seasonal crops
in rotation.

I eat well
so does Flora
she runs beside me
around the farm
checking the crops—
we run barefoot
past the windmill
solar powered
we run slow
past the hemp fields
the long strips
of cover crops
alfalfa
thick rows
of tall grasses
we run and run
pass the banana trees
the eggplant and cabbage
cauliflower, cucumbers
pineapples, wild fruit
berries, berries
we run by fat melon

bumpy balls
of juicy flavor.

I had to help
poor weak Donny
dig the hole
for my mother
I dug one
for him
after
made a life
for myself
by myself
scared
overwhelmed
a kid
worried
I'd be discovered
by the state
underage
no legal adult
no guardian
but somehow
I got overlooked
by the authorities
dealing with
the pandemics
the hurricanes
the floods
the sea rise
dead bodies
health emergencies
widespread crime
looting

abandoned buildings
closed roads
suicides
food shortages
rioting and
well,
you know,
it was a jungle
out there
so I elected
to hide out
in my own private
world, all
alone for years
and years
and now
I live well
in this overgrown jungle
wild land, the old farm
offering me riches
from the past.

I found a weathered sign
in the moldy kitchen
of the falldown
farmhouse
that said:
Farmlandia
and I repainted
the faded letters
hung it up
on the front gate.

One day I rescued
a small herd
of hungry goats
running wild
a few miles south
another day
somebody's grumpy pig
wandering the woods
Flora rounded them up
like she'd been doing it
all her life—
maybe she had.

We stand together now
at the backside
of the garden
while I scan
the red tomatoes
ripe, I pick
a handful
some green beans
a zucchini
a head of romaine.
*We're having a feast
tonight,*
I tell Flora
who looks like a deer
tan with white spots
on her flanks
she pants
her tongue pink
and healthy.

I don't have chickens

I would love eggs
poached, fried, scrambled
an omelet with fresh chives
but I still can't stand
the thought
of tending a coop
the smell reminding me
of factory lines
of death.

Chickens are omnivorous
they will eat anything
take care of themselves
I need to get past
my aversion
someday
but for now
I have goats
one big mean sow
her fat piglets
and Flora,
enough
mouths to feed
at Farmlandia.

We round the north side
by the kale and spinach
carrots and broccoli
onions, garlic, leeks
that taste of our dirt
our particular soil
like the goats
their milk has
terroir
like good wine

reflecting the land
the pastures
where they graze—
my goats eat well
clean grasses
rich and sweet.

Speaking of sweet:
the honey here
pure gold
luster
I'm not fond
of caring
for bees
for hives
but someone has to
appreciate
all the pollinators
in the blossoms
mouths full of buzz
colorful butterflies
cobalt blue, orange, striped
black and white
spiders that dine on
mosquitos and flies
the grasshoppers and beetles
kept at bay
with herbs
planted just so.

As Flora and I
head home
to deposit
the harvest litter

our garden birthings
I'm thinking of roots
how they reach in the soil
and cling, cling
I wonder if I will
ever
find someone
to help me
with farm work
I advertise online
but Florida
a no-man's land
no one knows
it's paradise found
here at Farmlandia.

I stop at the well
pump up
a pail of water
Flora slurps her bowl
I drink down
one cup, a second
thinking how
it took years
for the water supply
to lose a metallic
chemical taste
but now
it's fresh and wonderful.

Before we go inside
for breakfast
I breathe deep
the thick green air
that smells

like rot
like fertility
making me smile
the rich clean odor
of nature
of my life now
Farmlandia.

Flora and I
get our fill
of goats' milk
boiled oats
a drizzle of honey
a handful of raw fruit
before we head over
to the old farmhouse.

Last winter
I used up
all the old planks
nailed over
all the old windows
the old wooden shutters
rotted with humidity
I used
for firewood
and I ventured inside
the old farmhouse
for the first time
in years:
exploring
was amazing
amazing!

I fell in love
with the place.

My plan
to rehab the house
move in
tell myself
I'm modernizing,
but keep it old
historic
bring new life
to the original.

The trailer is damp
in heavy rainstorms
a sieve
and it still smells
like my mother—
which makes me sad
lonely and sad.
But the farmhouse
so ancient
it holds
no memories
for me
just an intrigue
with a distant time
unknown beauty
simplicity
functionality.

Flora circles twice
lies down
on the front porch
by the split-railing

covered with vines
purple morning glory
pearly white moon
fuchsia bougainvillea
her doggy tongue lolling
eyes wide, she pants
then rests her head
on padded paws
guards me
while I'm working

in the kitchen
on hands and knees
sanding rough pine
floorboards
lost
in a daydream
imagining
what life was like
in the early years
on the farm
in this house
in the fields
in the orchards
all the work
the chores
the animals
the hot humid days
the long dark nights
the inhospitable scrub
the snakes
the gators
the swarms of mosquitos
the harsh sun
the torrential rain

the droughts
the hurricanes
the floods
the rugged terrain.

The isolation.

Just like now!

Except for the grid
electricity
and a few other
modern conveniences
the way I live
almost the same as
how early settlers lived
how homesteaders lived
the women who lived
in this old farmhouse
on this old farm
their daily struggle
to survive
to grow enough food
to bear enough children
to pass on all they knew
to the next generation
with the hope
their lives
would be better
easier
less lonely
more rewarding.

I picture all the women
of Farmlandia:

sunburned women
hardened women
strong women
dark women
depressed women
weakened women
women milking cows
women gathering eggs
women planting gardens
women making meals
from scratch
women killing chickens
cooking them
on the potbellied stove
beside me.
I imagine the men:
big bodied men
hard muscled men
weather-beaten men
men drinking and fighting
men building and protecting
pushing
always pushing
to make the farm grow.

Flora barks soft
and I glance up:
two burrowing owls
cute brown twins
perched on the porch
railing, silent
big round eyes
staring at me
in sync

they swivel, fly off
into a whitewashed sky.

Smiling I turn away
moving slow
across the floor
smoothing it
perfecting it
for forgotten hours
as the sun moves
toward the drop slot
in the ever-changing sky.

For a moment
in the golden peach
twilight
clouds pink
mauve, tangerine
I want to say
out loud
how much I love
the land
how each day I think:
*Thank god
for Farmlandia!*

But that will be
a whole other story
I may share
one day—

but first
I must live it.

Sea Grape Jelly

3 cups sea grapes, mostly ripe
sugar
water

1. Half fill a large saucepan with ripe sea grapes. Add a few green ones.
2. Cover with water and bring to a boil; cook over medium heat until grapes are soft.
3. Mash grapes, put in a jelly bag; drain juice into a measuring cup, then measure out an equal amount of sugar.
4. Transfer grapes and juice to a saucepan; stir in sugar.
5. Cook over low heat until thickened enough that it jells on a spoon.
6. Pour into sterile jars and seal.

RECOMMENDED RESOURCES

Books on Florida History, Farming, and Regenerative Agriculture:

Wendell Berry, *The Unsettling of America*. Berkeley, CA: Counterpoint, 1996.

Gabe Brown, *Dirt to Soil: One Family's Journey into Regenerative Agriculture*. White River Junction, VT: Chelsea Green Publishing, 2018.

Loren G. Brown, *Totch: A Life in the Everglades*. Gainesville, FL: University Press of Florida, 1993.

Buena Carlson, *Farm Girl: A Wisconsin Memoir*. Madison, WI: University of Wisconsin Press, 2020.

Marjory Stoneman Douglas, *The Everglades River of Grass*. Sarasota, FL: Pineapple Press, 2016 (originally published in 1947).

Michael Grunwald, *The Swamp: The Everglades, Florida, and the Politics of Paradise*. New York: Simon & Schuster, 2007.

Kristin Kimball, *The Dirty Life: A Memoir of Farming, Food, and Love*. New York: Scribner, 2011.

Howard Kohn, *The Last Farmer: An American Memoir*. Lincoln, NE: University of Nebraska Press, 2004.

David R. Montgomery, *Growing a Revolution: Bringing Our Soil Back to Life*. New York: W.W. Norton, 2018.

David R. Montgomery and Anne Bikle, *The Hidden Half of Nature: The Microbial Roots of Life and Health*. New York: W.W. Norton, 2016.

Gary Mormino, *Land of Sunshine, State of Dreams*. Gainesville, FL: University Press of Florida, 2008.

Ken Mudge and Steve Gabriel, *Farming the Woods*. White River Junction, VT: Chelsea Green Publishing, 2014.

Tom Philpott, *Perilous Bounty: The Looming Collapse of American Farming and How We Can Prevent It*. London: Bloomsbury, 2020.

Theodore Pratt, *The Barefoot Mailman*. New York: Duell, Sloan and Pearce, 1943.
Tim Robinson, *A Tropical Frontier: Tales of Old Florida* (series). Indiantown, FL: Port Sun Publishing, 2020.
Upton Sinclair, *The Jungle*. New York: Doubleday, 1906.
Patrick D. Smith, *A Land Remembered*. Sarasota, FL: Pineapple Press, 1984.

Poetry on Farming, the Land:

Elizabeth Coleman, ed., *Here: Poems for the Planet*. Port Townsend, WA: Copper Canyon Press, 2019.
Audre Lorde, *The Selected Works of Audre Lorde*. New York: W.W. Norton, 1970.
Knud Sørensen, *Farming Dreams: Poems*. New York: Spuyten Duyvil, 2016.

Organizations for Information on Regenerative Farming:

Ecological Farming Association:
https://eco-farm.org/

Kiss the Ground:
https://www.kisstheground.com/

The Land Institute:
https://landinstitute.org/

Regeneration International:
https://regenerationinternational.org/

Rodale Institute:
https://rodaleinstitute.org/

Savory Network:
https://savory.global/

Sustainable Harvest International:
https://www.sustainableharvest.org/

FNR Foundation:
Check the Food and Nutrition Resources website for more links to information on changing the food system, improving agriculture practices, and empowering small farms and food workers:
https://fnrfoundation.org/resources.html

Recipes:

Travel Biscuits: Marjorie Kinnan Rawlings, *Cross Creek Cookery,* 1942 (as "Idella's Biscuits").
Sofkee: Mary Ulmer et al, *Cherokee Cooklore*, 1951.
Conch Chowder: Patricia Antman, *Florida Keys Cooking*, 1946.
Sweet Potato Pone: Florida Cracker Recipes, Florida Backroads Travel:
https://www.florida-backroads-travel.com/florida-cracker-recipes.html
Hoe Johnny: Florida Cracker Recipes, Florida Backroads Travel:
https://www.florida-backroads-travel.com/florida-cracker-recipes.html
Swamp Cabbage: Loren G. Brown, *Totch: A Life in the Everglades, 1993;* and Food Network (recipe from Davey Rauleson):
https://www.foodnetwork.com/recipes/swamp-cabbage-recipe-1914141
Sea Grape Jelly: Fort Lauderdale Historical Society, *Fort Lauderdale Recipes,*1964 (recipe from Mrs. Truman G. Lively):
https://www.sun-sentinel.com/news/fl-xpm-2013-04-16-qb-pioneerfood-story.html

ABOUT THE AUTHOR

Virginia Aronson is the executive director of Food and Nutrition Resources Foundation, a non-profit corporation that supports individuals, organizations, and communities actively seeking to improve access to healthy meals, nutrition education, regenerative agriculture, and a socially just food system. FNR has published three books of ecofiction: *A Garden on Top of the World*, *Bull Sugar,* and *Mottainai: A Journey in Search of the Zero Waste Life*, all from the European activist press Dixi Books. A poem from *Farmlandia* was nominated for a Pushcart Prize in 2020.

Healthy food, healthy children, healthy animals, healthy planet: fnrfoundation.org